Hey! You're back again! Oh, I get it. You want to see if you can outsmart the touted team of Rupert and Reginald, fairly famous for their Bible adventures. Well, think again!

But speaking of adventures, we have had our share since we last talked. Move over, Indiana Jones, Rupert and Reginald ride again! Let's see...there's a fiery duel, a battle of an entire army versus one man, an almost terminal ship- wreck, and, oh yes, the birth of a very special baby. You've heard of it raining cats and dogs? How about quails?!?

Of course, Reginald and I are up to our eyeballs in every adventure, or in Reginald's case, his beak. Always thinking of his stomach, Reginald has brought his birdseed into every adventure. True to form, he manages to lose it every time! See if you can find it. Also, there's a little Bible in every adventure. Once you find it, find the book, chapter, and verse (located under the adventure title) and read the adventure for yourself in your own Bible.

Time for us to check out, and you to get lost (in our all- new Bible adventures!).

Have fun!

Rupert

FIND RUPERT AGAIN

The FUN BIBLE SEARCH BOOK 2

CHAD FRYE

To two women who have fanned the flames of
enthusiastic support for their grandson:

Jeanette Grutsch Frye
Marjorie Lough Kihlgren

Titus 2:3-5

A Barbour Book

The First Skyscraper

Genesis 11:1-9

After the great flood only Noah and his family lived on the earth. Now, a long time later, thousands of people are around! But instead of living in many cities, the people built one great city. With bricks made from mud, the people were even building a tower to reach to the sky! God knew if the people lived together the world would become very bad again, so God caused the people to speak different languages. No one could understand each other and the tower was never finished.

Find Rupert, Reginald, Reginald's bird-seed, the little Bible, and the things highlighted below.

Clipboard

Coffeepot

Adam's apple

Wagon

Tool belt

It's Raining Quails?!?

Exodus 16; Numbers 11:4-35

Moses had led the people of Israel out of Pharaoh's Egypt and slavery. Now they were on their way to a land God had promised them, but the desert journey was not easy. At first God sent them bread from the sky but now the Israelites wanted meat. God gave them what they wanted, *and* what they deserved. God sent so many quails the people became sick of them! God wanted the people of Israel to trust and worship Him.

Find Rupert, Reginald, Reginald's birdseed, the little Bible, and the things highlighted below.

Net

Bird stew

Bulging eyes

Slingshot

Bird in a beard

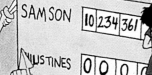

SAMSON 10 234 361

PHILISTINES 0 0 0

Lethal Weapon, B.C.: A Donkey's Jawbone

Judges 15:9-20

Samson, the strongest man in the Bible, and the Philistines, Israel's fiercest enemy, were not exactly friendly. Now the Philistines were out for revenge, but they were in for a surprise. Incredibly, Samson allowed himself to be tied up in heavy ropes. As soon as the Philistines got close enough, guess what happened? Samson ripped off the ropes and, using only the jawbone of a donkey as a weapon, killed almost a thousand men! God gave Samson superhuman strength to rule Israel.

Find Rupert, Reginald, Reginald's bird-seed, the little Bible, and the things highlighted below.

Dynamite detinator

Hot Dog

Samson

News reporter

Small sword

A very small muscle

A Bad Hair Day

2 Samuel 17:24 - 18:33

Absalom was a son of King David who wanted to be king himself. Together with his own army he fought his father's soldiers: He would have to win a battle to become king. Absalom's last battle was fought in a deep and dangerous forest called the Wood of Ephraim. While King David's soldiers won the battle, Absalom rode away on his mule, hoping to escape. Instead, his long hair became tangled in the branches of an oak tree and his mule ran off! Absalom would never be king.

Find Rupert, Reginald, Reginald's bird-seed, the little Bible, and the things highlighted below.

Tickling

Small bunny

Absalom

Keys

Rock dropper

Climber

Joab

Elijah Under Fire

1 Kings 18:17-40

God's prophet Elijah was tired of messing around. There is only one God and he wanted everyone to believe him! Elijah challenged the prophets of the idol Baal: They would build two altars with an animal sacrifice on top. The one true God would set fire to the sacrifice. Baal's prophets screamed and cut themselves. Nothing worked. Elijah was confident. He ordered twelve barrels of water poured over his sacrifice. God's fire burned up the water, the bull, and the stones! Many people then believed in God.

Find Rupert, Reginald, Reginald's birdseed, the little Bible, and the things highlighted below.

Mustache tied in a bow

Multipurpose knife

Elijah

Old man

Handkerchief

Switchblade

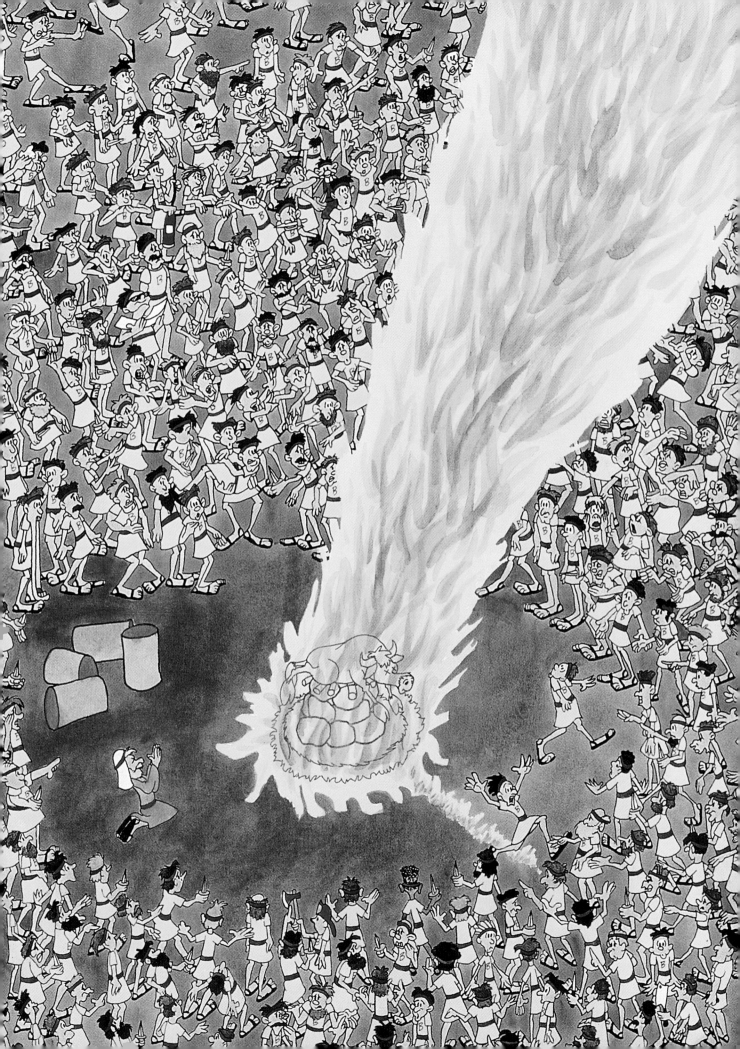

A Table For Four (Lepers)?

2 Kings 6:24 - 7:20

The people of Samaria were in trouble. They had no food and, worse than that, their arch enemies, the Syrians, were camped outside their walls. Still Elisha, God's prophet, told Samaria's king that they would soon have food! How? Four men with a disease called leprosy decided to beg for food from the Syrians. But when they went to their tents, the Syrians were gone. God had scared them away! Now the Samaritans could feast on the food of their enemy.

Find Rupert, Reginald, Reginald's bird-seed, the little Bible, and the things highlighted below.

Stilts

Beehive hairdo

Sneaker

4 Lepers

The king

Skateboard

SYRIAN CAMP
we're rough,
tough,
& hard to bluff

Jesus Is Born!
Luke 2:1-21

The Roman emperor ordered everyone in Israel to return to the towns of their ancestors to pay taxes. Although Mary was almost ready to give birth to God's Son, Jesus, she and her husband Joseph had to go...to a place called Bethlehem. Bethelehem was so crowded that Mary and Joseph stayed in a stable, beside cows and sheep! That very night Jesus was born, and on a nearby hillside angels shouted the news to shepherds. The King of the world had been born!

Find Rupert, Reginald, Reginald's birdseed, the little Bible, and the things highlighted below.

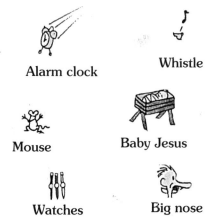

Alarm clock

Whistle

Mouse

Baby Jesus

Watches

Big nose

Fishers of Men

Matthew 4:18-22; Mark 1:16-20; Luke 5:1-11

The day had started out like any other day for these fishermen. Peter and Andrew were out in their boat fishing; James and John were mending their nets, a necessary task. All of a sudden, Jesus approached them and asked them to follow Him. And they did, right away! They left their fishing, their families, and their homes because the Son of God needed their help. Jesus would spend a short time on earth and he needed to tell as many people as possible about God's love for them.

Find Rupert, Reginald, Reginald's birdseed, the little Bible, and the things highlighted below.

String of fish

Andrew

Peter

John

Old salt

Jesus

James

Up On The Roof!

Matthew 9:1-8; Mark 2: 1-12; Luke 5:17-26

Jesus was in the city of Capernaum and, as usual, crowds of people were around him. One man crippled with palsy—he could not walk—had friends carry him to the house where Jesus was staying. But when he got there the room was so crowded, the man could not enter. Desperate to see Jesus, the man was then carried up to the roof. The roof was then cut open and he was let down on his bed right before Jesus! Jesus healed the man because he believed in Him.

Find Rupert, Reginald, Reginald's bird-seed, the little Bible, and the things highlighted below.

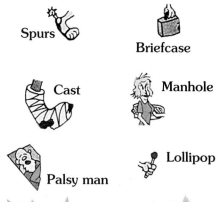

Spurs

Briefcase

Cast

Manhole

Lollipop

Palsy man

MELVIN'S DELI

Shout Hosanna!

Zechariah 9:9; Matthew 21:1-11;
Mark 11:1-11; Luke 19:28-44;
John 12:12-19

Was it really Jesus? Oh yes, there He was, riding a donkey, entering the city of Jerusalem! People began waving palm branches and cheering "Hosanna!" (In the Hebrew language hosanna means "Save us, we pray.") The people wanted Jesus to be their king. A group of religious leaders called Pharisees had other ideas. In a few days Jesus would be labeled a criminal and sentenced to death. Jesus was and always will be our king because He is God's Son.

Find Rupert, Reginald, Reginald's birdseed, the little Bible, and the things highlighted below.

Headband

Baby carriage

Saddle shoes

Kissing

Jesus

Yellow bottle

Zap! What Happened To Zacchaeus?

Luke 19: 1-10

Nobody liked tax collectors! When they collected money for the government often they charged too much...and kept the extra money for themselves! That is what Zacchaeus did, until he met Jesus. One day Jesus came to the city of Jericho and Zacchaeus, who was short, climbed a tree to see Him. Jesus knew Zacchaeus was in the tree and He told him to come down. Jesus wanted to go to the home of a tax collector! After that day, Zacchaeus gave back all the money he had stolen.

Find Rupert, Reginald, Reginald's bird-seed, the little Bible, and the things highlighted below.

Woodpecker

Zacchaeus

Beanie

Groundhog

Goose crossing sign

Jesus

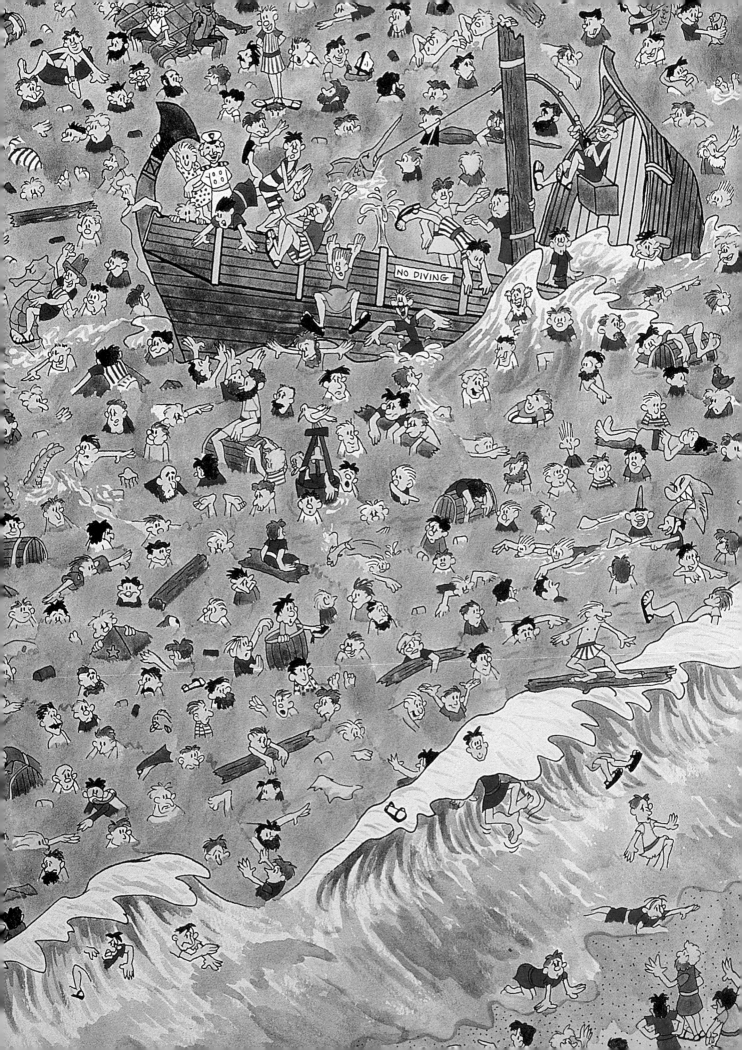

Paul Is Shipwrecked

Acts 27:1 - 28:11

Because Paul couldn't stop telling others about Jesus, he was taken prisoner. Now Paul was on a boat bound for Rome where he would be judged by Caesar, the ruler of Rome. Suddenly a terrible storm arose and great crashing waves nearly broke the boat apart. Hanging on for their lives, the passengers threw heavy loads overboard to make the ship lighter. But an angel of God told Paul that everyone on board would be saved. At the end of fourteen days land was sighted and everyone swam ashore.

Find Rupert, Reginald, Reginald's bird-seed, the little Bible, and the things highlighted below.

Horseshoe crab

Periscope

Viper

Buoy

Paul

Water wings

The First Skyscraper

1. Pizza
2. Tattoo
3. Shopping basket
4. Radioactive barrels
5. Red work gloves
6. Limbo
7. A stick in the mud
8. Ruler
9. Pencil

Lethal Weapon, B.C.: A Donkey's Jawbone

1. Rubber band
2. Football
3. Sunglasses
4. Platform sandles
5. Pro wrestler
6. Firecracker
7. Sword in the stone
8. Wallet
9. Coin toss
10. Chinese star
11. White flag

Jesus is Born!

1. Yearbook
2. Water faucet
3. Flowers
4. Candle
5. Drum stick
6. Hand bell
7. Beggar
8. Pickpocket
9. Soldier

Fishers of Men

1. Cat eating a fish
2. Parrot
3. Wig
4. Crow's nest
5. Spider
6. Pet octopus
7. Cotton candy
8. Hook hand
9. Crab on an ear
10. Newspaper
11. Fish bones
12. "It was thiiis big."

Up on the Roof!

1. Meter man
2. Spitting camel
3. Paperboy
4. Catching a bull by the horns
5. Flat wheel
6. Double-parked horse
7. Wheelchair
8. Street musician
9. Fire hydrant
10. Doorbell

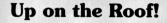